Power Rhythm Guitar

31 lessons for rhythm guitar by yourself, in a band, or as a back-up musician.

By Ron Middlebrook with Dave Celentano

The CD was recorded by Dave Celentano
and engineered by Devin Thomas
at Southwest Sound in
Sierra Madre, California

ISBN 0-931759-96-X
SAN 683-8022

Copyright © 2018 CENTERSTREAM Publishing
P.O. Box 17878 - Anaheim Hills, CA 92817

www.centerstream-usa.com | centerstrm@aol.com | 714-779-9390

Contents

FOREWORD

This book will cover various methods and techniques to play rhythm guitar by yourself, in a band or as a back-up musician.

Let's start from the beginning. First the strum should suit the song. Think about it. You wouldn't want to play a country rhythm to a hard rock song, would you? Consider the song style first, and the rhythm will follow.

The rock rhythm guitar player must back his singing or the other band members with drive, push, force, strength, and character. If you are just starting out, avoid the rhythm patterns that are too complex, just keep it simple, but keep it steady and on time.

Keeping time means the rhythm is constant, playing steadily, straight ahead rhythm giving the music solid foundation.

THE PICK-STRUMMING HAND

Your strumming hand is where it's at! It's the initiator of the sounds
from your guitar. The attack of the strumming hand generates the
energy, drive and percussiveness of the guitar.

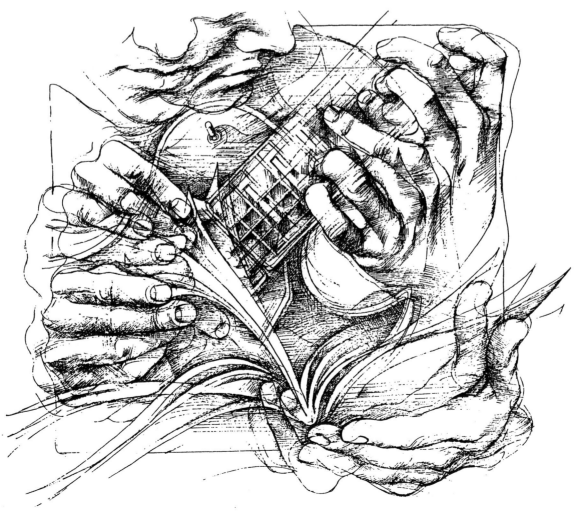

BASIC CHORDS USING OPEN E POSITIONS

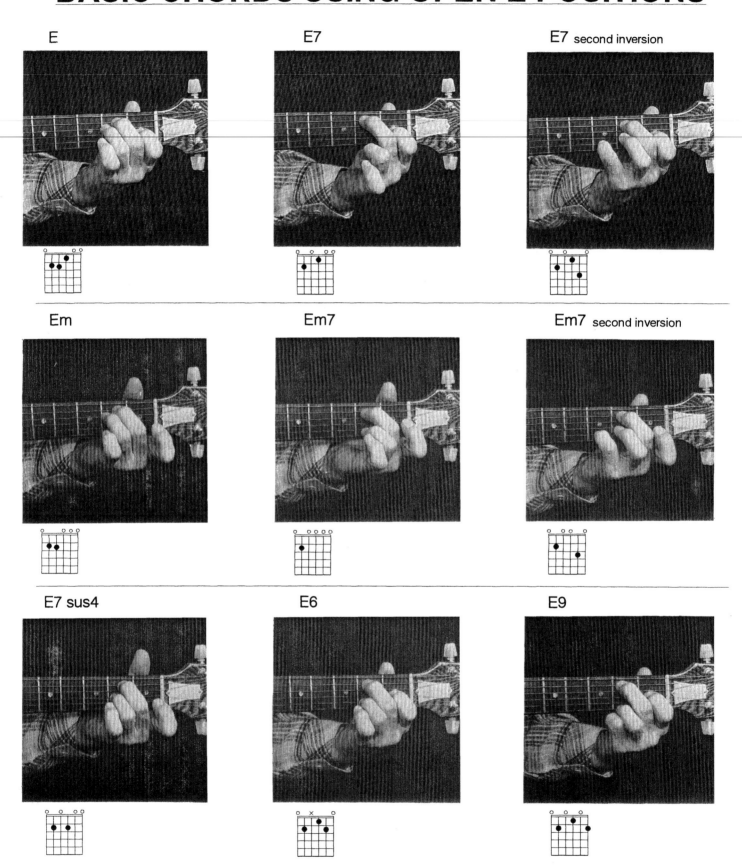

The ROOT of a chord is the fundamental note upon which the remainder of the chord is built.

The ROOT is the letter name given to a chord, i.e. the ROOT of G7 is G, the ROOT of Cm7 is C, EbMaj.7 is Eb, etc.

HOW TO PLAY BAR CHORDS

Your first attempt at the bar chords might make you want to put the guitar down and never pick it up again.

It goes something like this; your pressing down as hard as you can and the strings either buzz or they sound like rubber bands. Your thumb feels like it's going to fall off. Your forearm is starting to ache. Remember we all started out the same way.

Just keep practicing them, pretty soon you'll be playing them clean and fast.

HERE'S SOME GOOD RULES TO FOLLOW FOR
ALL CHORDS, BUT BAR CHORDS ESPECIALLY:

1. Keep your barring finger off the fret you're on.

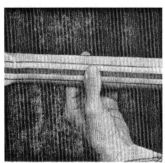

2. Put your thumb in the middle of the neck, keeping it straight.

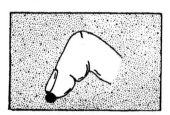

3. Arch your other fingers, so they don't touch the strings underneath them.

4. Keep the fingertips close to the frets as close as possible, without touching, otherwise the proper pressure and leverage are lost, and strings will buzz.

One other thing, the higher the strings are off the fretboard, the harder it's going to be to press them down on the frets. If you feel the strings are too high, take your guitar to a guitar repair man to have the strings lowered.

BAR CHORDS USING E FORMS

The root name of the chord will be found on the sixth (6) string.

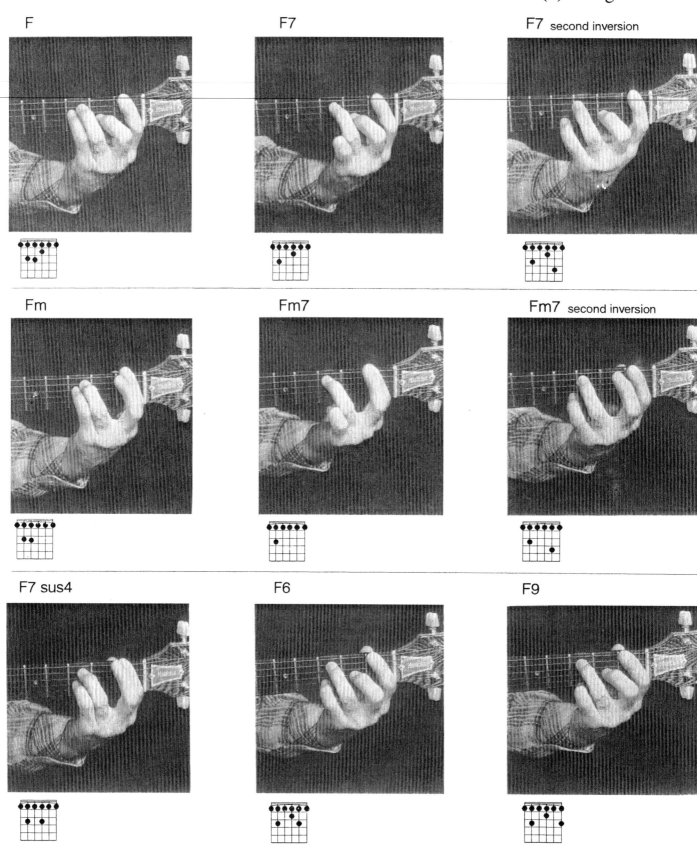

For an in-depth chord study, look for Ron Middlebrook's book,"The Illustrated Guitar", published by CENTERSTREAM.

LOCATE THESE CHORDS
(Using E Forms)

Use the 6th string to find the root.

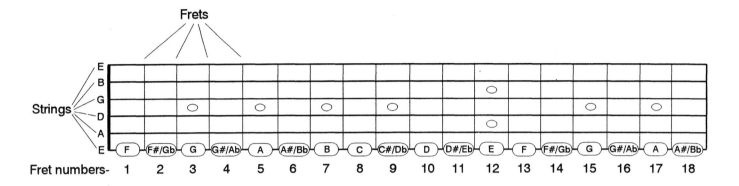

Use this guide to locate the other bar chords.

Example: If you want to play a G chord, simply move the F bar chord up the neck, stop on the 3rd fret, which is G and there you have it. Bb (B flat)? Simple! Move up to the 6th fret, etc.

A7	Am7	C
G	Ab7	Ebm
Ab7sus4	G6	F#m7
Bb9	Gm	F6
C#7	A7sus4	Dm7
G7	Bb	C6
F	D	Bm7
Bm	A#m7	Db7

BASIC CHORDS USING OPEN A POSITIONS

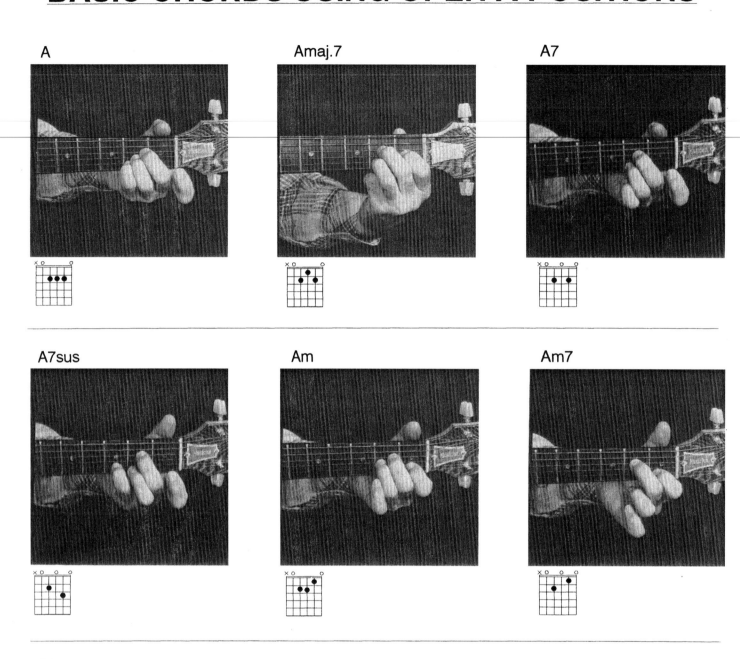

A   Amaj.7   A7

A7sus   Am   Am7

A6

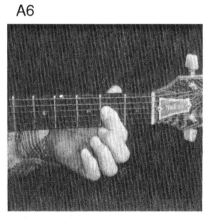

BAR CHORDS USING A FORMS

The root name of the chord will be found on the fifth (5th) string.

Bb

Bbmaj.7

Bb7

Bb7sus4

Bbm

Bbm7

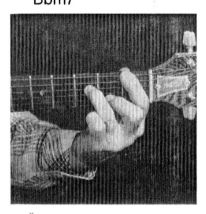

Bb6

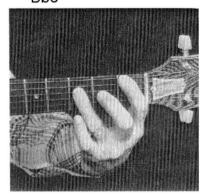

LOCATE THESE CHORDS

(Using A Forms)

Use the 5th string to find the root.

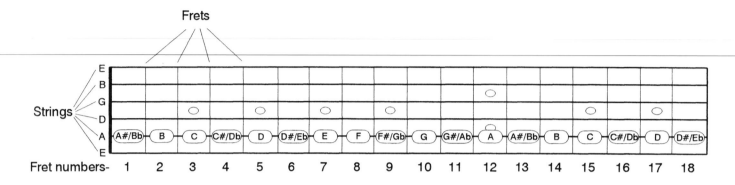

Use this guide to locate the other bar chords.

Example: If you want to play a C chord, simply move the Bb bar chord up the neck, stop on the 3rd fret, which is C, and there you have it. How about Dmaj7? Simple! Move up to the 5th fret and bar the maj.7 form.

C	F#maj.7	Fm7
Db	Ab7	Ebm
Cm7	G6	F#m7
Emaj.7	Gm	D7sus4
C#7	A7sus4	Dm7
G7	Bb	C6
Dm7	C#6	Bm7
Bm	A#m7	Db7

LOCATE THESE CHORDS
USING BOTH E AND A FORMS
Use all bar chords.

G	Cmaj.7	F#m7	Ebmaj.7
form- (E)	(A)	(E)	(A)
Abmaj.7	**Bbsus4**	**C#7**	**C6**
(E)	(A)	(A)	(E)
Fm7	**G6**	**Bbsus4**	**C#sus4**
(A)	(E)	(A)	(E)
C7	**Fsus4**	**Absus4**	**D**
(A)	(E)	(E)	(A)
Dbmaj.7	**Dbm7**	**Bb6**	**D7**
(E)	(E)	(E)	(E)
Ab	**Cm7**	**Em**	**Emaj.7**
(E)	(A)	(A)	(A)
F7	**A7**	**G7**	**A6**
(A)	(E)	(A)	(E)
Bb	**B7**	**G**	**Eb7**
(E)	(A)	(E)	(A)

INTRODUCTORY FUNDAMENTALS

1. STAFF

The staff is a set of FIVE horizontal lines (with four spaces between) each of which are used to designate a specific pitch.

2. TIME SIGNATURE or METER SIGNATURE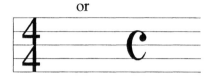

The TIME SIGNATURE or METER SIGNATURE is the set of numbers at the beginning of each musical composition. The BOTTOM number tells WHAT KIND of fundamental notes will make up each measure, while the TOP number tells HOW MANY of these there will be in each measure. The 4/4 time signature is often called COMMON TIME and indicated in the music with a "C".

3. MEASURE or BAR

The MEASURE or BAR is the grouping of musical notation between two vertical lines on the staff with their placement derived according to the time signature.

4. REPEAT SIGN

The REPEAT SIGN means to return to the beginning and play the same music once again or repeat from the last repeat sign inverted in the opposite direction and play again.

5. TEMPO

TEMPO is the rate of speed at which a musical composition is to be played. For general playing, it should ALWAYS be kept very steady.

6. METRONOME

A METRONOME is a timing device that can be regulated to work at a variety of INDIVIDUAL speeds. By listening to its "clicking" pulse, the ability to play at a STEADY tempo can be developed.

USING THE METRONOME

Only allow the metronome to pace your progress by practicing at a tempo setting at which you make no mistakes. Then gradually increase the tempo as your ability to perform the strums develope.

I've notated the down and up strums that work for me. Feel free to adjust them as you see fit. Keep in mind downstrokes seem to have more force and are always stronger than upstrokes.

INTRODUCTION TO THE
RHYTHMIC NOTATION SYSTEM

The rhythmic notation system is a MATHEMATICAL "sign language" that tells WHEN to play and WHEN NOT to play. It is based on the division of ONE whole note or rest into its elementary fractional parts which include: TWO halfs, FOUR quarters, EIGHT eighths and SIXTEEN sixteenths. Each of these notes and rests is allowed a specific number of counts or a fractional part of one count which corresponds with its value. Memorize each of the notes and rests shown below with their appropriate time values.

Notes

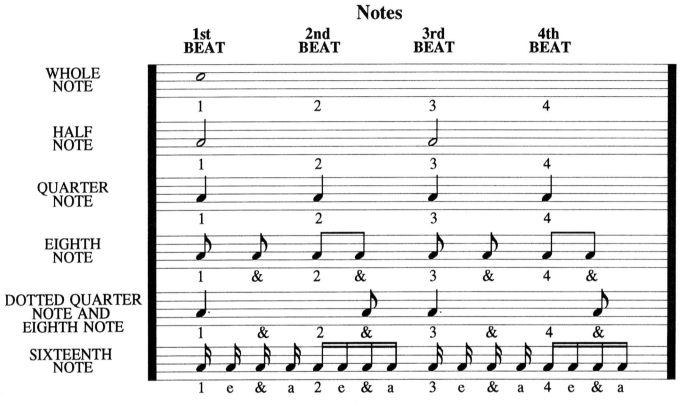

Hearing rhythms involves more than just hearing notes. Hearing where notes aren't, the spaces, and rests, are equally important. Below are the rest signs.

Rests

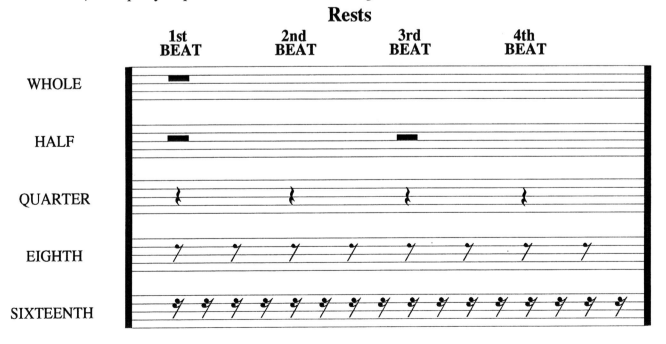

COUNTING RHYTHMS
RHYTHM, EVERYBODY HAS IT

A tight sense of rhythm can and does make the difference. It's not just a matter of talent- it's a product of our efforts. Below are a set of exercises to give you practice in counting out the various rhythmic patterns. Use any note on the guitar or even an open string. Count aloud and try tapping your foot. Start out slow. *Accuracy, not speed is important.*

Reading music notation is not the aim of this book, we're just reading time values. However, I strongly urge you to learn music notation if you don't know it, as it's a valuable tool to communicate with other musicians.

KEY TO THE SYMBOLS USED

Down strum

Up strum

Accent: emphasize the accented strum by strumming them slightly harder or louder. This is notated by a circle around the accented beat.

A curved line that connects two strums together is called a tie. The first strum is struck and *held* for the value of both strums- *the second strum is not played.*

Rhythm slash mark for a quarter note strum. The full chord is strummed as one beat. These slashes will also be used for eighth note and sixteenth note rhythms.

Whole note rhythm mark. Strum the chord once and let ring for four beats.

Mute or deaden the chord fingering hand (see muting on lesson 18.)

Measure repeat sign (bar repeat). Means repeat previous measure one time.

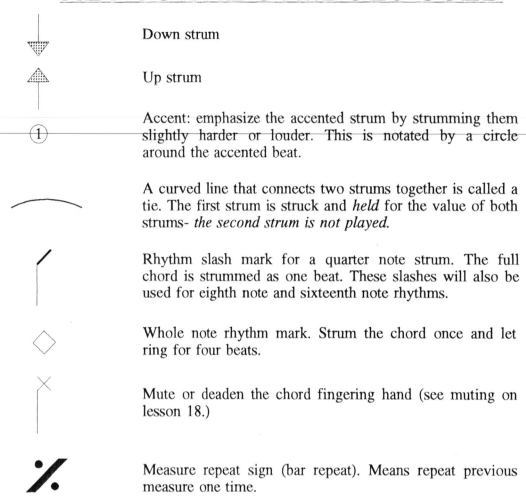

TABLATURE

Horizontal lines = strings (6= low E, 5= A, 4= D, 3= G, 2= B, 1= high)
Numbers on the lines = frets to place fingers on

G Major bar chord (all strings strummed at same time)

Strings

Frets (play one note at a time)

SYNCOPATION

Syncopation is a well known rhythmic device involving the shifting of a musical accent or stress point, so that it temporarily displaces the normal accent pattern.
One of the most direct is either to play a strong beat where a weak beat should fall or to play a weak beat where a strong one would normally fall.

RHYTHM LESSON 1

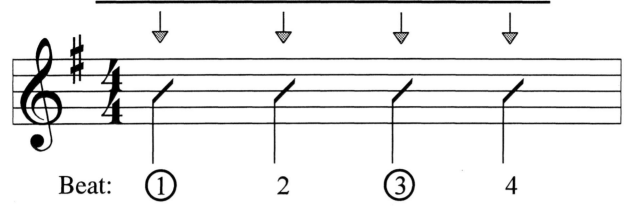

Beat: ①   2   ③   4

Strum all strings down. Each strum recieves one beat. The accent is on the 1st and 3rd beat.

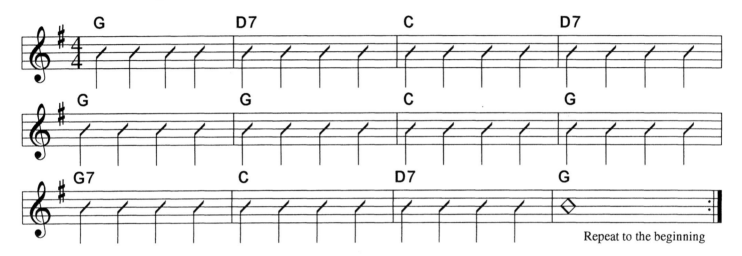

Repeat to the beginning

RHYTHM LESSON 2

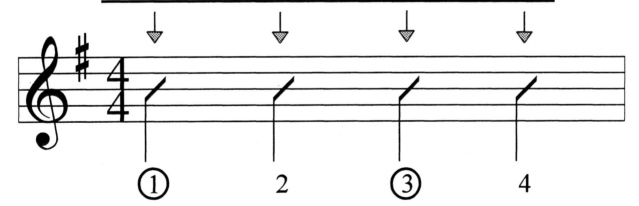

①   2   ③   4

Same pattern as lesson 1, but this time the rhythm is more active with two chords per bar.

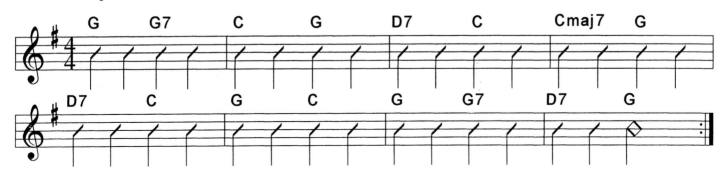

RHYTHM LESSON 3

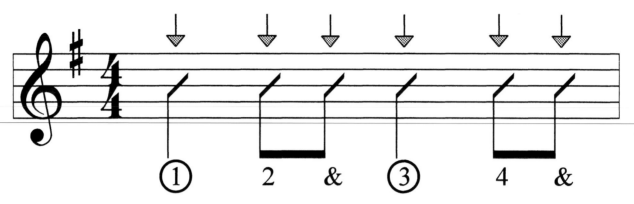

On this lesson we take the 2nd and 4th beats and *divide them in half.* We're still playing four beats, but on the 2nd beat we play two strums twice as fast and same on beat 4. Use all down strums.

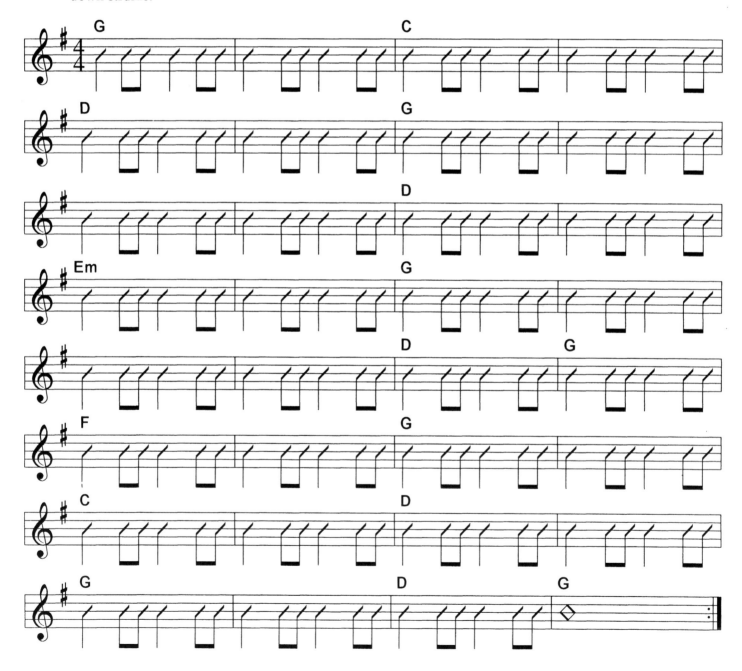

RHYTHM LESSON 4

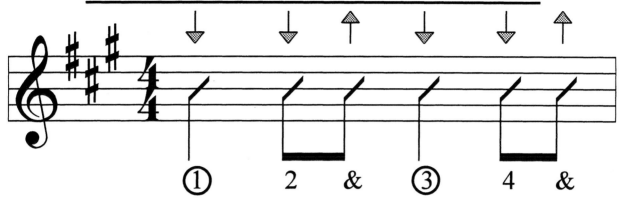

Same pattern as Lesson 3, but notice the *UP* strums on the last half of beats 2 and 4. Also the chords are more active with two per bar.

Use all bar chords

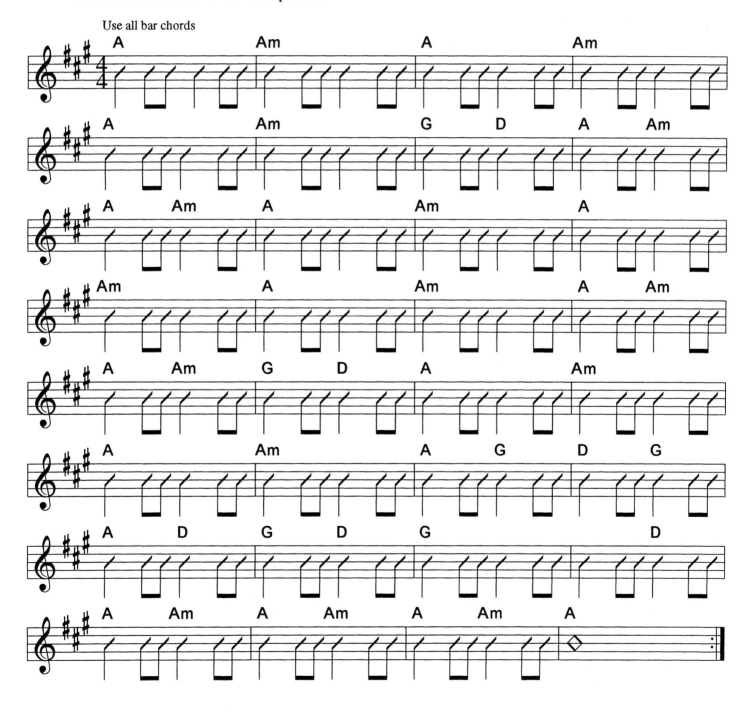

RHYTHM LESSON 5

3/4 TIME

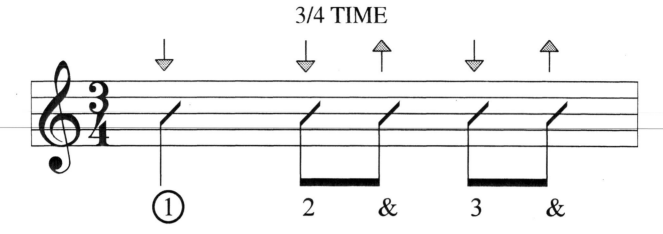

This one is in 3/4 time. Notice the accent only on the first beat, and there are only three beats per bar.

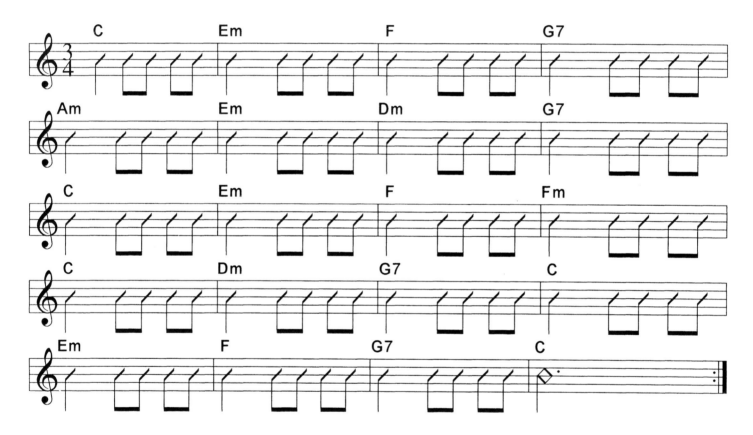

RHYTHM LESSON 6
BASIC ROCK

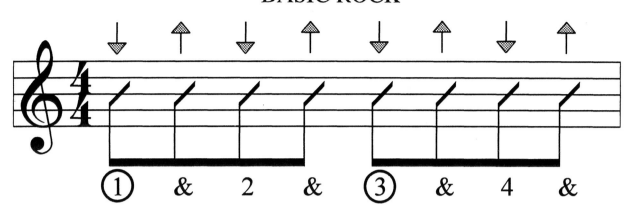

This is a basic eight note strum with the accents on the 1st and 3rd beats. Notice that this strum has alternate down and up strokes.

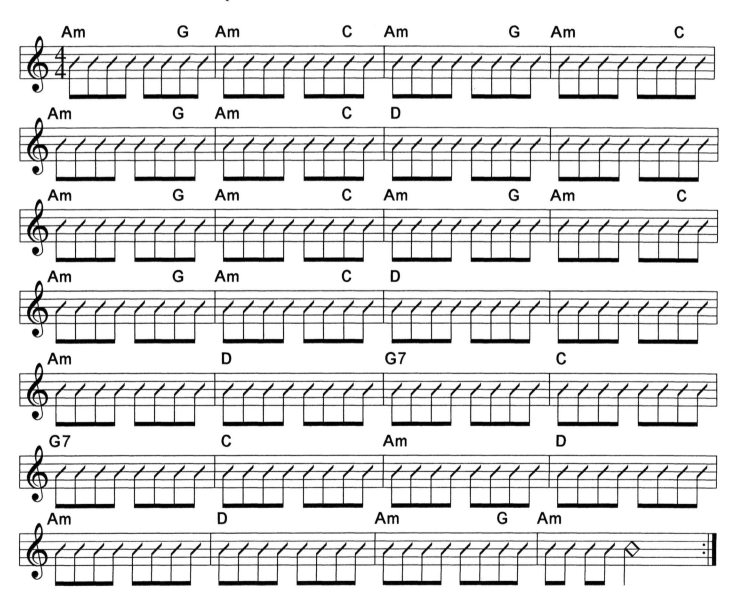

Start out slow. As you become more comfortable with the various patterns and as you begin to speed up, the counting will fall away and the rhythm will carry you along.

RHYTHM LESSON 7

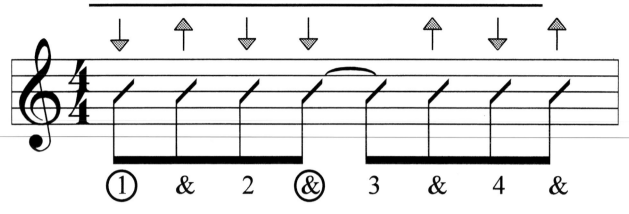

Same basic eight note pattern with a few exceptions. Notice the accent on the 1st beat and on the last half of the 2nd beat, *which is strummed down*. Also the tie over the first half of beat 3.

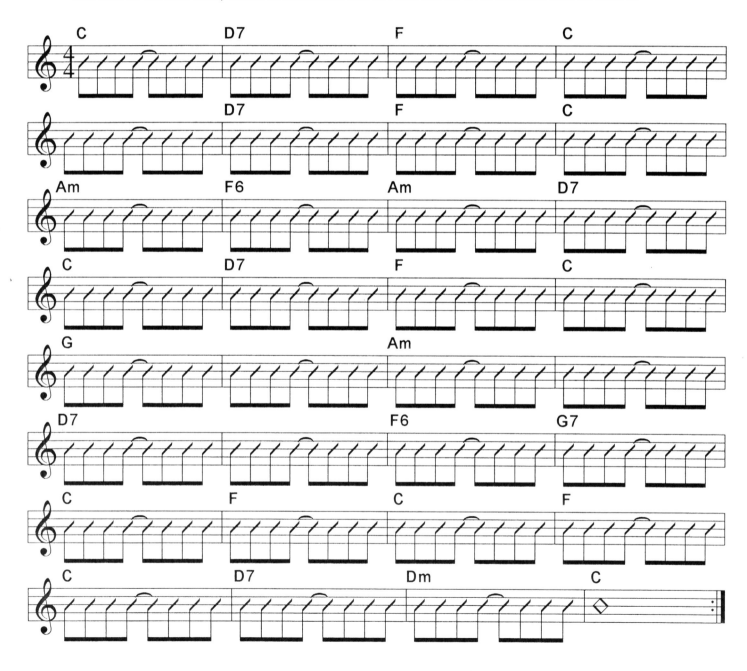

LOCATING THE RHYTHM PATTERN
ON SHEET MUSIC

Most sheet music will have no specific rhythmic pattern for guitar. We're left to our own devices to create an interesting rhythm pattern. All we're given is a word or two that suggests the tempo. See example 1.

Example 1

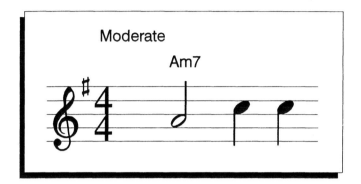

Occasionally, there will also be a metronome setting for the tempo. See example 2.

Example 2

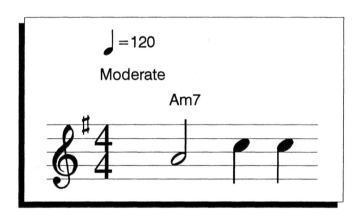

Here are some of the more common words you'll see:

Moderately Fast Blues
Moderately Slow
Moderately Fast Rock Beat
Moderately Slow Rock Beat
Slow Blues
Moderate Rock Beat
Brightly
Slowly
Fast
Moderately Slow, with a beat

RHYTHM LESSON 8
COUNTRY /ALTERNATING BASS NOTES

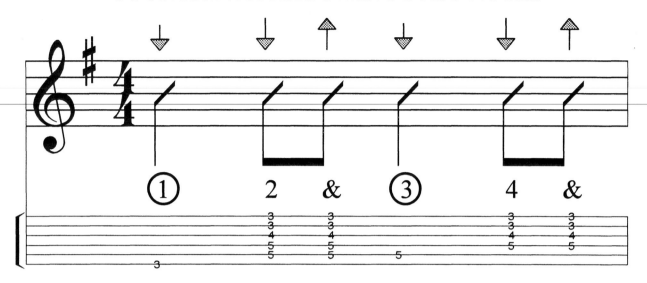

Country rhythms often use alternating bass notes. Hit the bass notes with a short down strum on beats 1 and 3. Give the chord a full down and up strum on the 2nd and 4th beats.

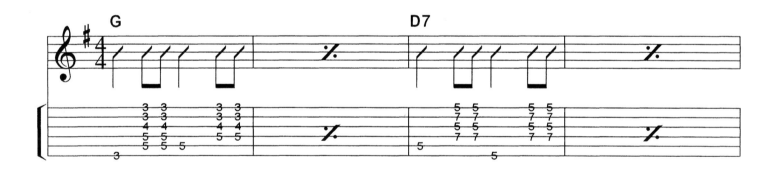

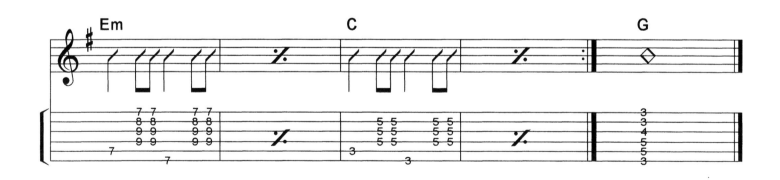

RHYTHM LESSON 9
COUNTRY /ALTERNATING BASS NOTES AND PASSING NOTES

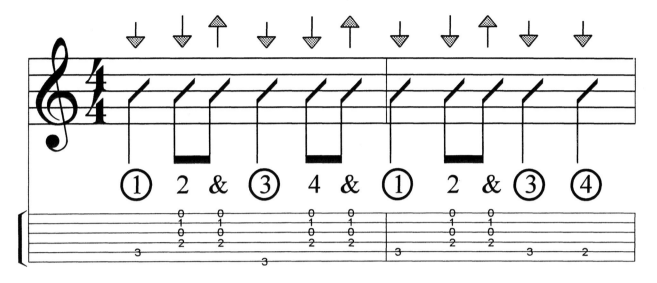

Same as the last exercise, except this uses *passing notes* to ease the transition between chords. Sometimes these passing notes are referred to as walking bass lines. A little tricky, but cool sounding.

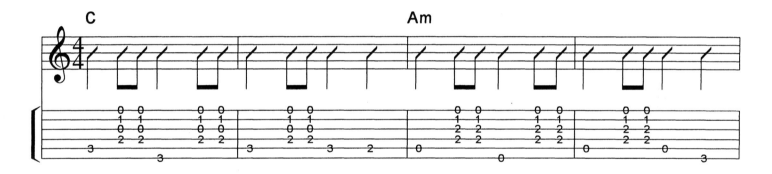

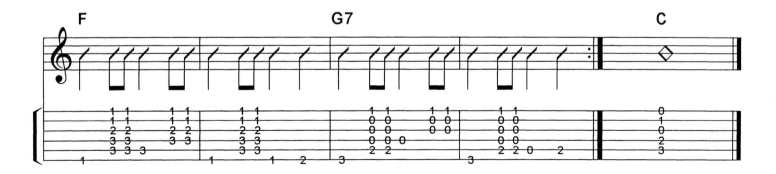

RHYTHM LESSON 10
LIGHT ROCK BALLAD

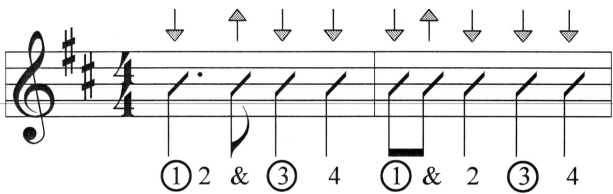

A two bar pattern. The dotted quarter on the 1st beat and eighth note on the last half of beat 2 is a little tricky. Notice almost all down strums except on the & of beat 2 (1st bar) and the & of beat 1 (2nd bar).

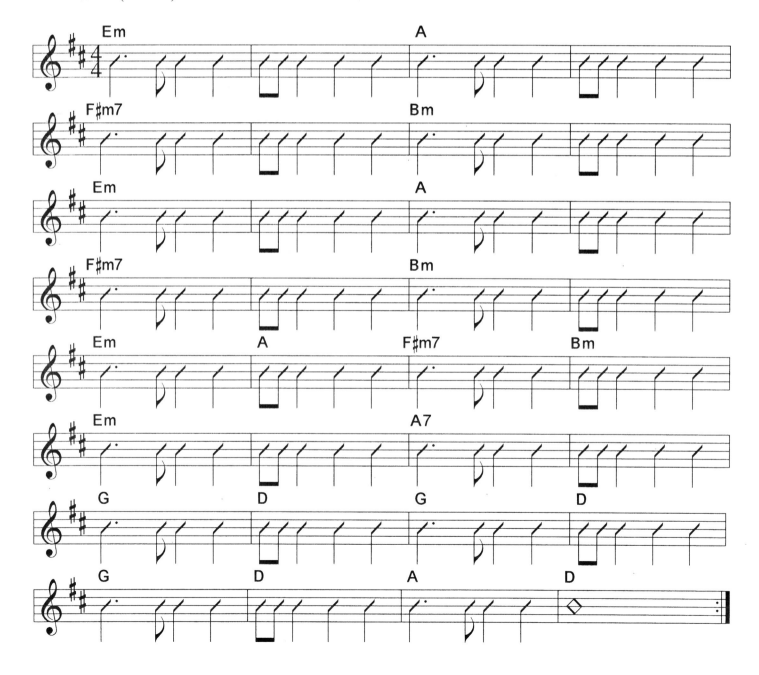

POWER CHORDS

You don't have to play all six strings to play good rock rhythm guitar. Sometimes it's not even desirable. One of the important functions of the rhythm guitarist is accenting the music in various ways. Using "power chords" is one way.

Sometimes in music they will be written this way: "G5". Study the photos below to play power chords and then play the pattern on the next page.

G5 (no 3rd)- 3rd fret

-3rd fret

C5 (no 3rd)- 3rd fret
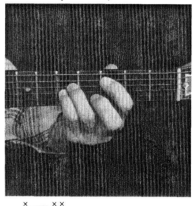
-3rd fret

D5 (no 3rd)- 5th fret
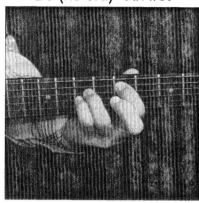

-5th fret

Mute or deaden the strings not being played with the front of the index finger. This may take some practice. Just let the finger lightly touch the strings, so they don't ring if accidentally struck.

A5 (no 3rd)- 5th fret

-5th fret

E5 (no 3rd)- 7th fret

-7th fret

F5 (no 3rd)- 1st fret

-1st fret

27

RHYTHM LESSON 11
HARD ROCK WITH POWER CHORDS

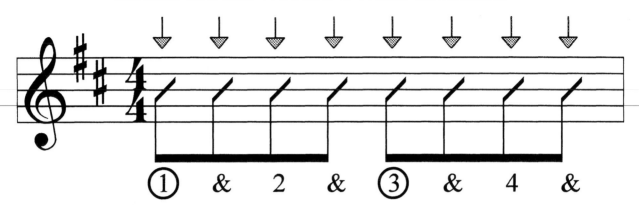

This rhythm has a hard driving sound using all 8th notes, all down strums and accents on the 1st and 3rd beats.

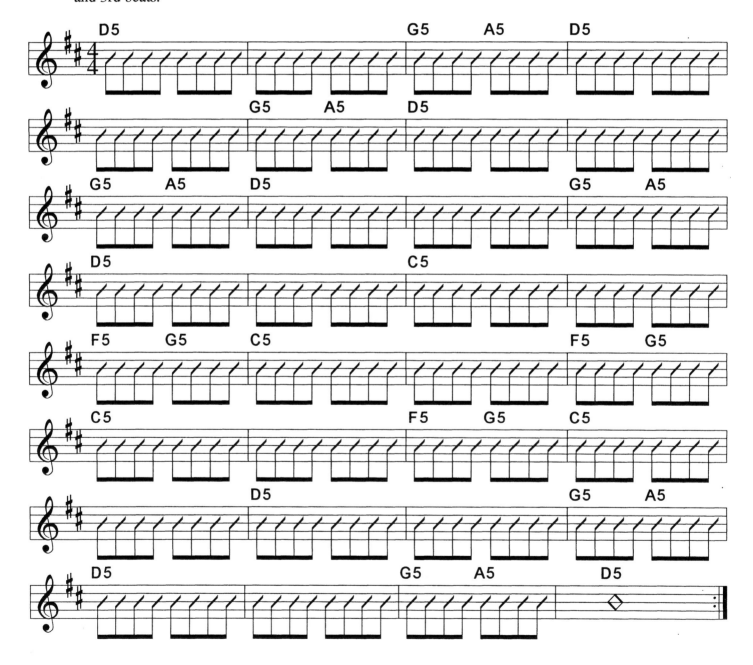

RHYTHM LESSON 12
HARD ROCK WITH POWER CHORDS

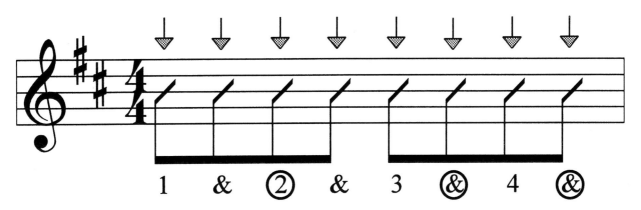

1 & ② & 3 ⓐ 4 ⓐ

Same as previous lesson, except the accents are on beat 2, the & of beat 3 and the & of beat 4. Keep the all the down strokes steady and just play the accents a little harder. This type of accenting pushes the rhythm more.The hard rock/ punk band GREEN DAY uses this type of rhythm often.

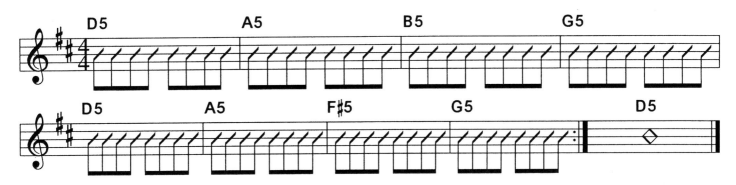

RHYTHM LESSON 13
HEAVY METAL WITH POWER CHORDS

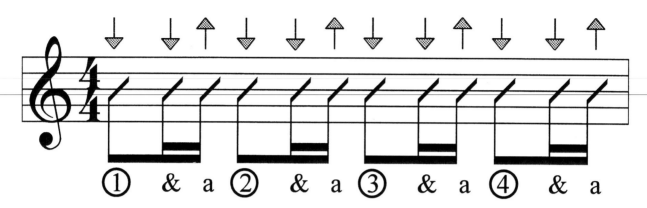

Introducing 16th note rhythms. 16th notes are connected by two horizontal beams and are played twice as fast as 8th notes. This rhythm sounds like a horse gallop if you can play it fast enough. It's got to be IRON MAIDEN's favorite rhythm. More of their songs use this than I can shake my pick at!

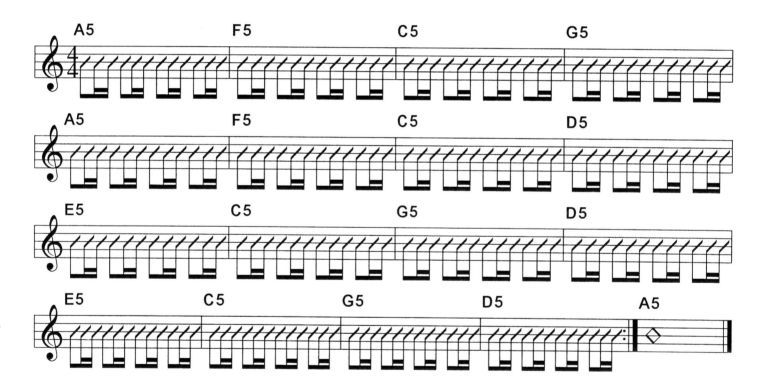

RHYTHM LESSON 14
HEAVY METAL WITH POWER CHORDS

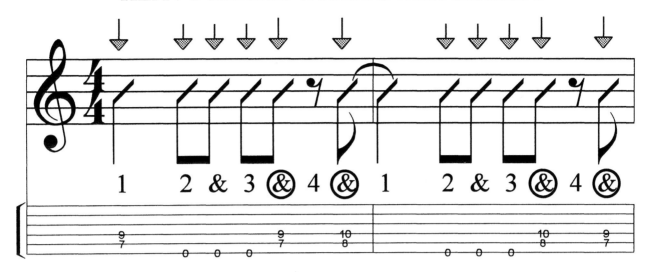

Two new ideas in this lesson. First, play the power chords with just the first and third fingers, omitting the fourth finger. You might find it easier to move the chords around this way. Second, the open low E string as a *pedal tone*. Try palm mutting the low E string by placing the palm (heel) of the picking hand on the strings between the bridge and the first pickup. This gives the rhythm a chunky sound used a lot in heavy metal.

RHYTHM LESSON 15

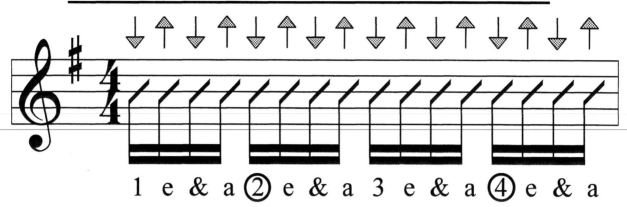

1 e & a ② e & a 3 e & a ④ e & a

Here's a rhythm using all sixteenth notes. It's just eighth notes played *twice* as fast. Notice it's all down and up strumming. Accents on the 2nd and 4th beats.

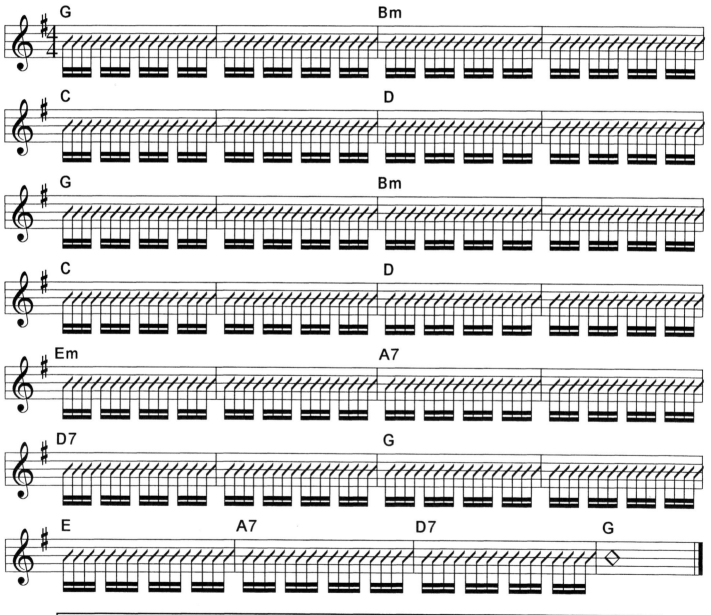

Rhythm players with a good sense of time are in demand. Keep your playing steady and even.
Working with a metronome is a big help.

RHYTHM LESSON 16

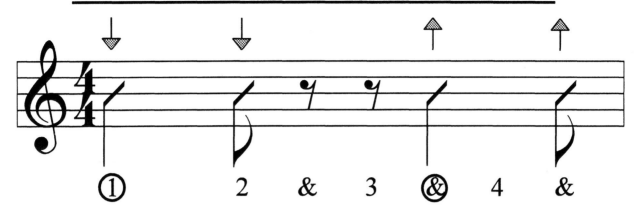

One of the most popular rock patterns. Look for the rest on the last half of the 2nd beat and the first half of the 3rd beat.

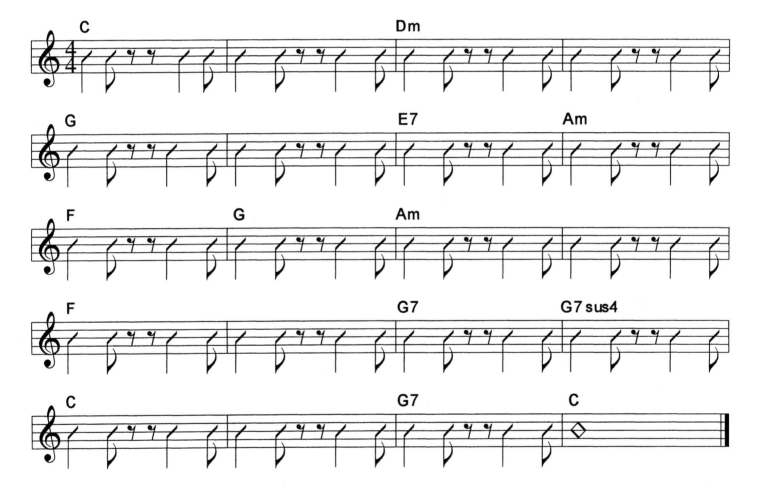

MUTING

When a chord or note is muted, it doesn't sustain or ring out. Instead all you get is a dull, deadened sound.

There are two ways of muting:

1.) Using the fleshy part of your palm (heel) on the strumming hand. Check out lesson 14 for this type of muting.

2.) Using the fretting hand (the hand that plays the chords). Slightly release the pressure from your hand, but don't take your fingers completely off the strings. Now strum the chord and you should hear the muted sound.

Study the pictures below and use the second method of muting for lessons 17, 19 and 20.

FINGERS PRESSED DOWN

FINGERS RAISED

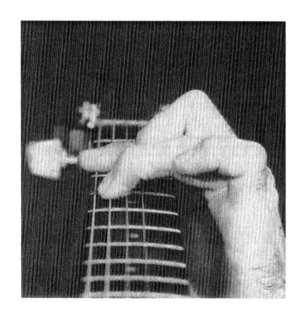

FINGERS PRESSED DOWN

SIDE VIEW

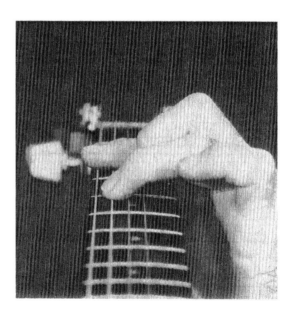

FINGERS RAISED

SIDE VIEW

RHYTHM LESSON 17
MUTING WITH BAR CHORDS

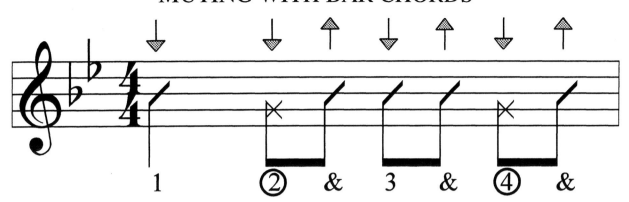

Here we have the muting effect on the accented down strums of beats 2 and 4. Use the second muting technique. Remember to release the finger pressure of the chording hand to get the muted sound.

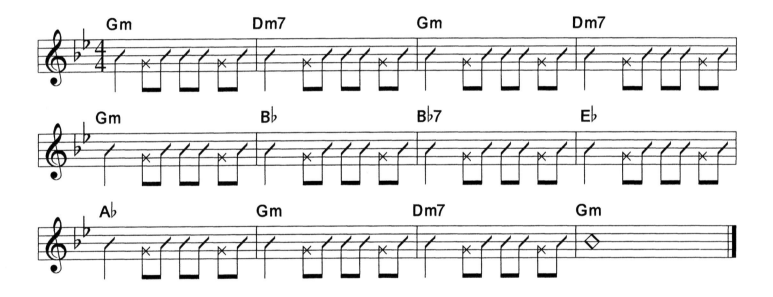

RHYTHM LESSON 18
RAGGAE

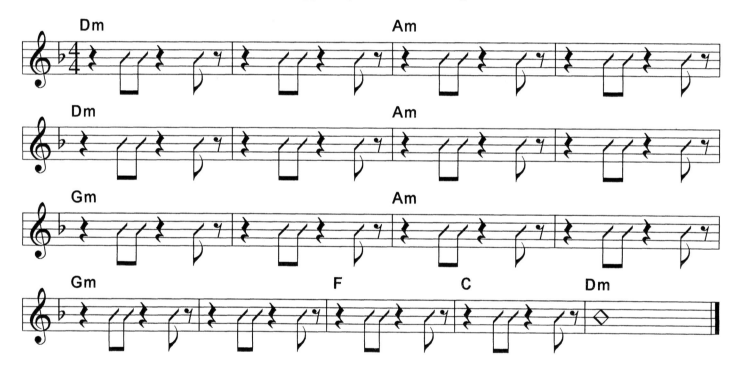

Raggae guitar is played sparsely. The accents are on beats 2 and 4. With the exception of the up strum on the & of beat 2 nothing else is played. Bob Marley help make this style popular and the rock band The Police even use Raggae rhythms in their songs.

RHYTHM LESSON 19
RAGGAE AND MUTING

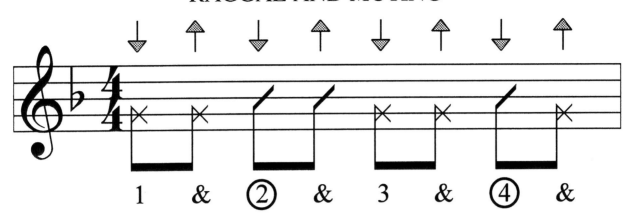

Same rhythm as the previous, but here we'll explore muting instead of rests. This fills out the rhythm a little more.

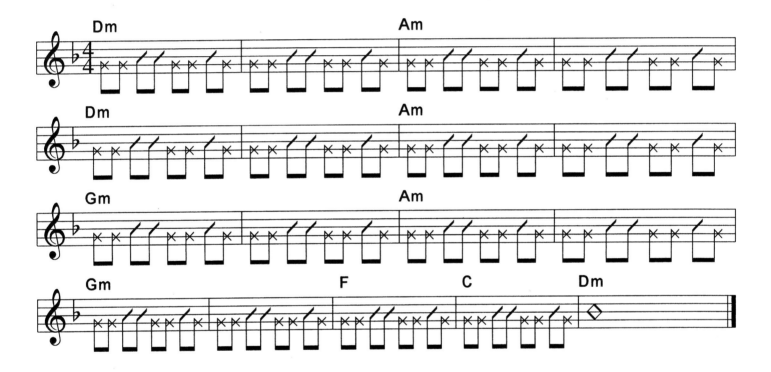

RHYTHM LESSON 20

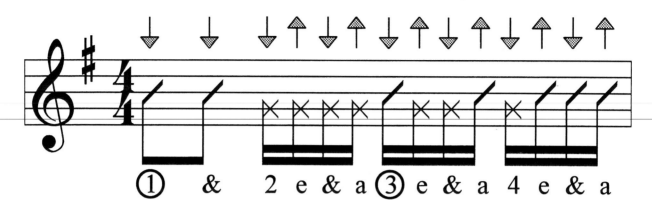

Grunge rock band Stone Temple Pilots use muted rhythms like this one below. Practice this syncopated rhythm slowly at first, then gradually speed it up.

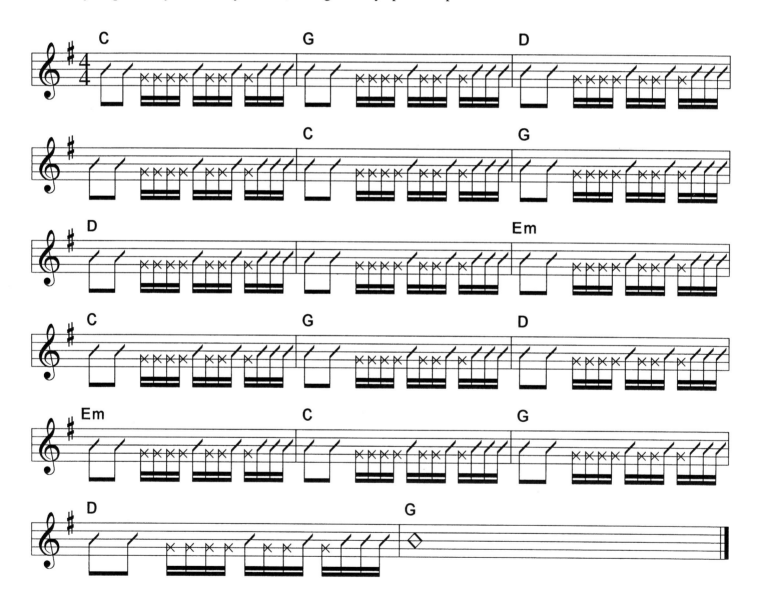

RHYTHM LESSON 21

PETE TOWNSHEND STYLE ROCK

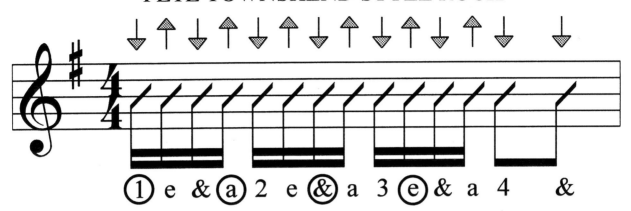

Here's a Pete Townshend style rhythm. Much of Pete's rhythm work was based off the accents.
On this example play steady down and up strums while accenting the circled ones.

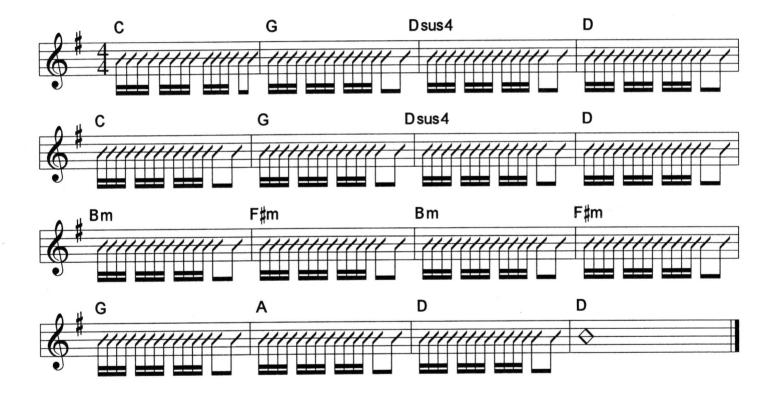

RHYTHM LESSON 22

PETE TOWNSHEND STYLE ROCK

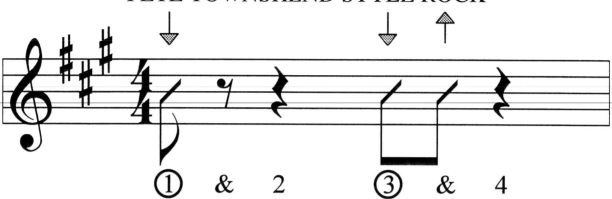

Here's a Pete Townshend style rhythm using the powerful rhythmic tool *less is more*. The guitar cuts through and lets the music breathe by playing less. It's played almost exclusively on the accents. Be sure to stop the chords from ringing during the rests.

RHYTHM LESSON 23

LIGHT ROCK

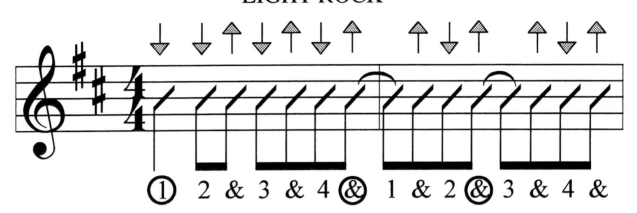

Notice the accented strums on the last half of beat 4 in the first bar and the last half of beat 3 in the second bar.

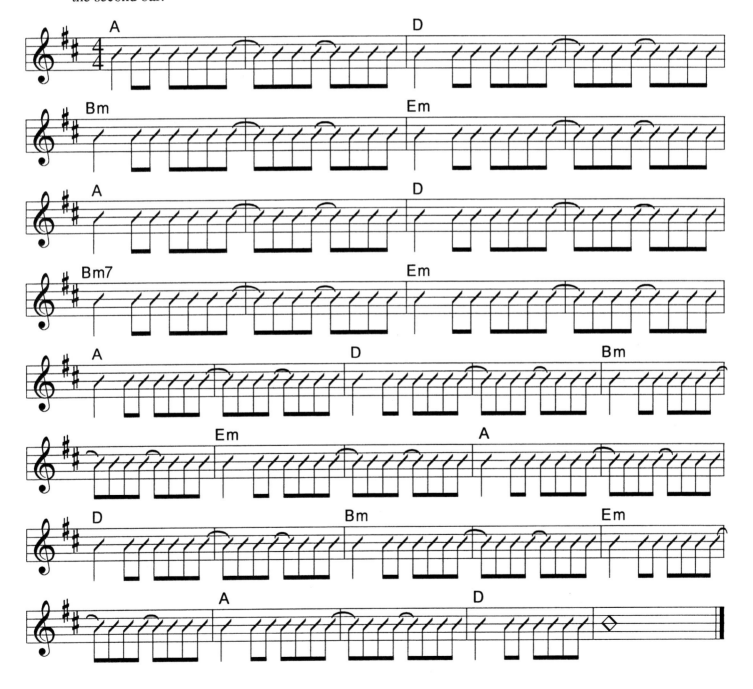

RHYTHM LESSON 24
LIGHT ROCK / HARD ROCK

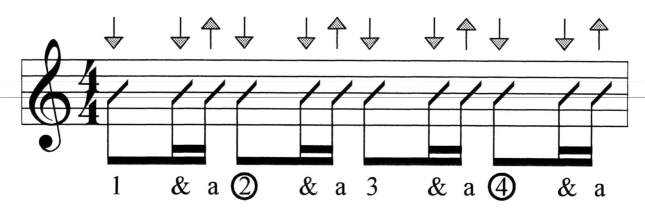

This rhythm is very common. Played slowly it works as a nice acoustic strum, but speed it up and you've got a classic heavy metal rhythm. Iron Maiden uses this *horse gallop* rhythm often.

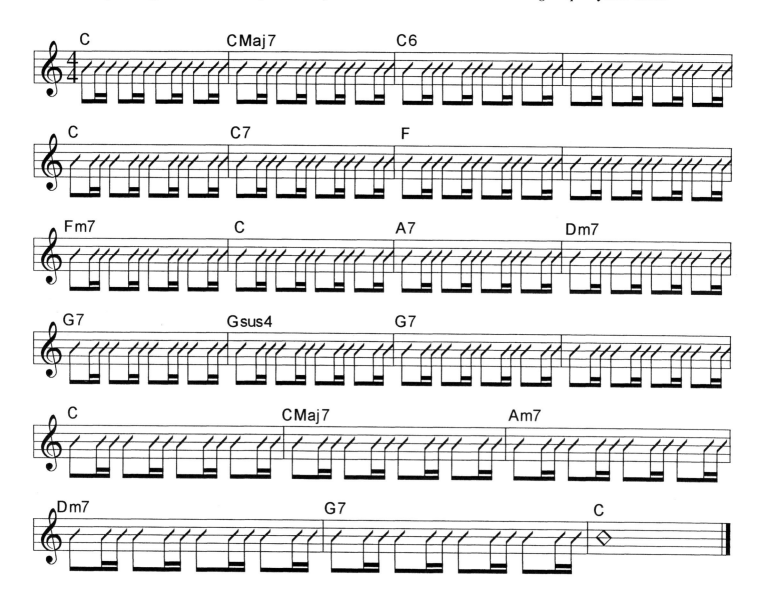

RHYTHM LESSON 25

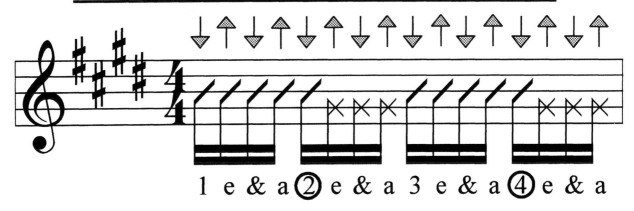

1 e & a ②e & a 3 e & a ④e & a

Straight ahead sixteenth notes, accents on the 2nd and 4th beats. Just lightly release the pressure from the chords for the muted parts.

43

RHYTHM LESSON 26
FUNK

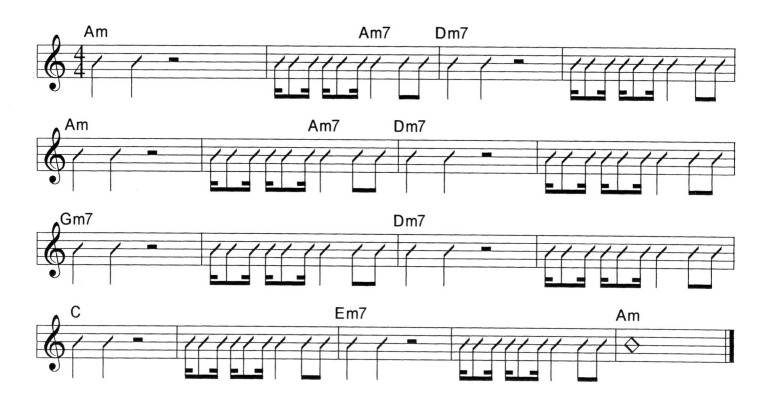

Here's a two bar rhythm figure. The two beat rest in the first bar leaves a musical gap to be filled in by other instruments or a vocal line. Watch the upstrokes on the accented parts of beat 1 and 2 in the second bar.

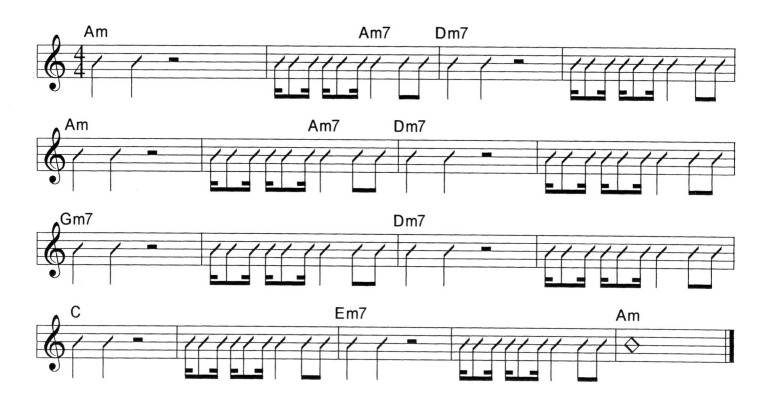

Rehearse these strums to that level of performance which does not require your conscious thinking about the techniques involved. You reach this level first by gaining a total awareness of the moves involved and second, by ingraining the moves into a habit. Only at this level of habit can these strums be automatically recalled and implemented without effort.

RHYTHM LESSON 27
FUNK

1 e a 2 e & a 3 e a 4 e & a 1 e a 2 e a 3 4 &

Look out for the muting in the first bar. Notice if you divide the first bar in half, the first and second half are the same. Also, the second bar is the same as the second bar of Rhythm Lesson 26.

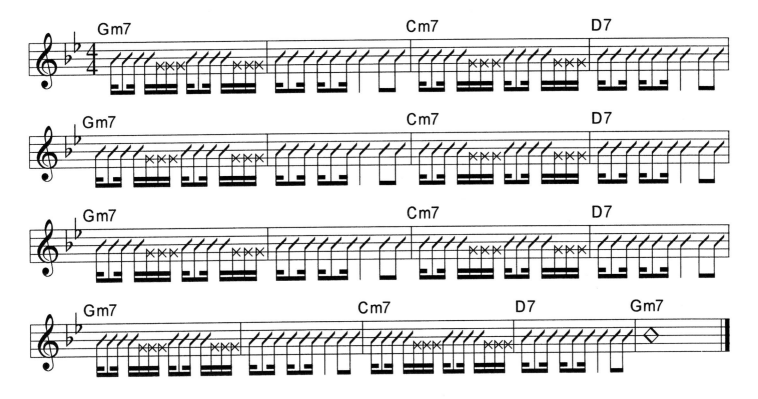

RHYTHM LESSON 28

CHUCK BERRY STYLE

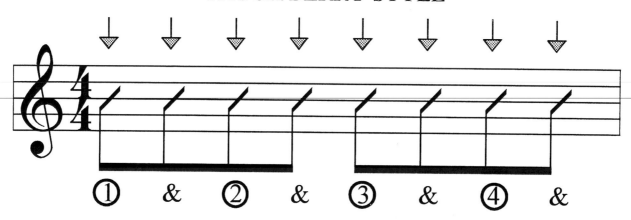

The most important part of the Chuck Berry style is consistency in picking. Each strum is a strong power strum, so use *ALL DOWN STRUMS*. Only two strings are to be played for each step.

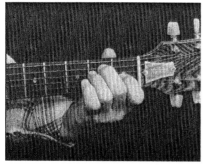

STEP 1
Form the E chord, pick only the E and A strings (6 & 5) together two times.

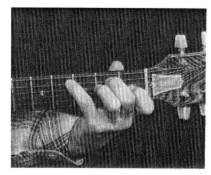

STEP 2
Place little finger left hand at the fourth fret of the fifth string. And again strike the E and A strings (6 & 5) together two times.

STEP 3
Repeat steps 1 and 2.

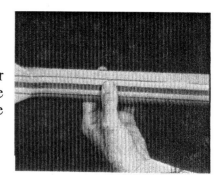

If the reach of your little finger is too difficult, check your thumb placement. It should be centered on the back of the neck. And try lowering your thumb a little more to the High E (first) string.

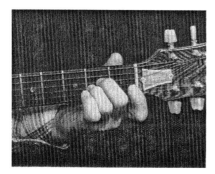

STEP 4
Form the A chord and pick only the A and D strings (5 & 4) together two times.

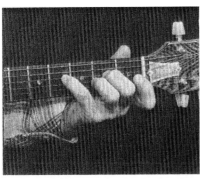

STEP 5
Place your fourth finger at the fourth fret and again pick the A and D strings twice.

STEP 6
Repeat steps 4 and 5.

STEP 7
Go back to E chord and repeat steps 1 and 2 four times.

STEP 8
Form the B power chord as shown in the photo at left. Pick the A and D strings twice.

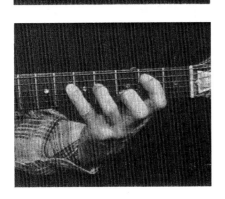

STEP 9
Place your fourth finger on the fourth string at the sixth fret and again pick the A and D strings twice.

STEP 10
Repeat steps 8 and 9.

STEP 11
Repeat steps 4 and 5 (A chord) twice.

STEP 12
Repeat steps 1 and 2.

STEP 13
Strum the B7 chord down twice (from the fifth string down).

Emphasize the bass strings. We want to sound like a rhythm guitarist and bass player playing together.

It would be a good idea to listen to some of the different variations in tempo which Chuck Berry has recorded, paying careful attention to the accents of the beats.

RHYTHM LESSON 29
CHUCK BERRY STYLE

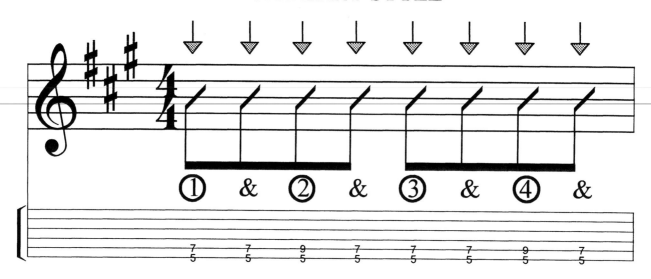

Here's a variation on the Chuck Berry style from lesson 28. Use power chords with the first and third fingers and reserve the fourth finger for the added note on beats 2 and 4. Use all down strums and only hit the two strings that your fingers are on.

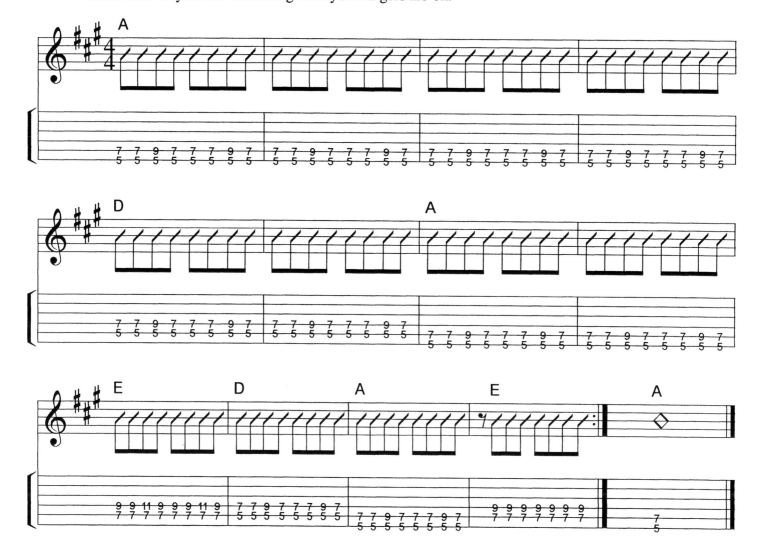

RHYTHM LESSON 30
BLUES

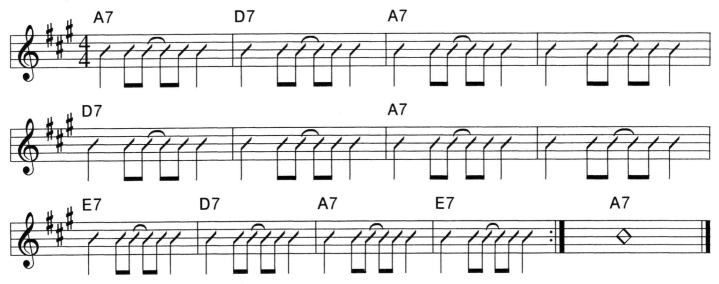

① 2 &③ 3 & 4

This is a *twelve bar blues* progression, a favorite of Stevie Ray Vaughn. It's the same as the last two lessons, but use all 7th chord bar chords. The strum accents are on beat 1 and the & of beat 2.

A7   D7   A7

D7   A7

E7   D7   A7   E7   A7

RHYTHM LESSON 31

JAZZING UP THE BLUES

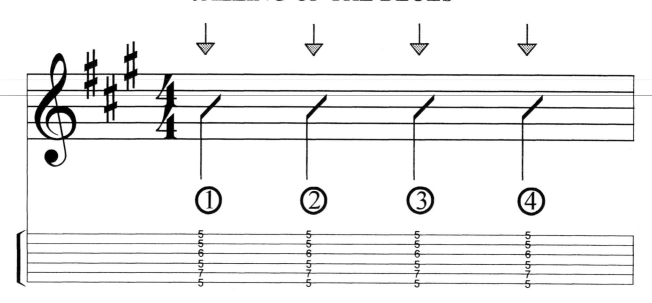

A standard 12 bar blues progression just like lesson 30. By adding the different chord substitutions the pattern has a more jazzy feel. If we play a quick, sharp down strum on each beat, this will give us a 1930's swing feel. The Allman Brothers also helped make this rhythm popular.

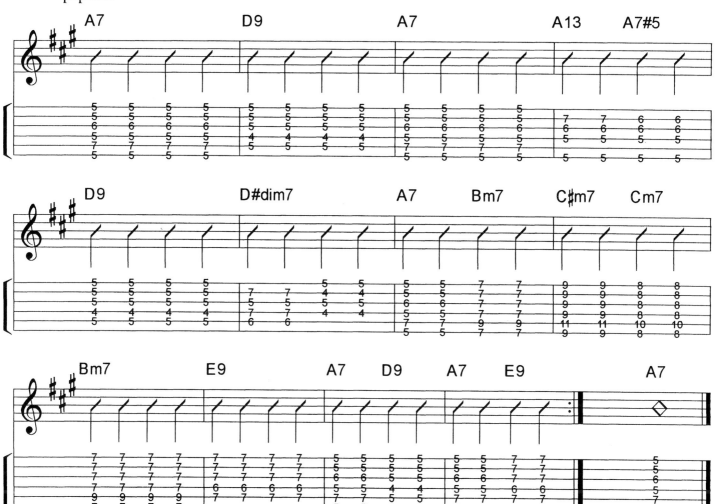

FINAL NOTE ON PLAYING RHYTHM GUITAR

Even if you're a lead guitarist, you'll be playing rhythm guitar more often in the song. Think about it. A typical song is about ninety percent rhythm and ten percent lead.

The ability to read chord charts is imperative. No doubt you'll encounter an altered chord once in a while. Here's what a few altered chords might look like: E7#9, A7b9 or D7#5. This is easier to read and play than it looks.

First you must master the three basic chord types discussed earlier in this book: major 7, minor 7 and dominant 7. You should know how to play all three types with the root on the 6th string and root on the 5th string. Next, understand that the alterations (#5, b9, #9, etc.) refer to flatting or sharping that particular scale degree in the chord. Take D7#5 for example: play a D7 chord, find the fifth scale degree (count up the D major scale to the fifth note, which is A) and sharp it (raise it one fret). Do E7b9: play E7, find the ninth scale degree (count up the E major scale to the ninth note, which is F#) and flat it (lower one fret). Here's how to play these two chords:

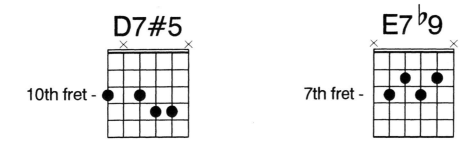

Practice figuring out other chords. It's pretty easy once you get the hang of it. Good luck!

CONCLUSION

These are not the only rhythms in the world. For different rhythms, try combining other patterns. Make up some of your own. Keep a log of your new rhythms by writing them down on paper or recording them. Good rhythms make the difference between an amateur and professional guitarist. You make the choice.

BIO

Dave Celentano is a graduate of Musicians Institute (G.I.T.) in Hollywood, California. He's the author of numerous guitar method books, cassettes, CDs and videos. Currently, Dave's teaching guitar in the Los Angeles area at Dr. Music, Grayson's Tunetown, Gard's Music and Pasadena City College.

For a free catalog of all Dave's books, cassettes and CDs write to:

Flying Fingers Music
c/o Dave Celentano
P.O. Box 1994
Arcadia, CA 91077-1994

Photo by Lawrence Photography

More Great Guitar Books from Centerstream...

ASAP POWER PICKING
For Electric and Acoustic Guitars

by David Brewster This book will help beginning guitarists "find" the strings of the guitar through a series of basic (yet melodic) picking exercises. As you become more comfortable striking the strings of the guitar with a pick using the exercises and examples here, you should eventually create your own variations and picking exercises.

00001330 Book/CD Pack.................................$15.99

LATIN STYLES FOR GUITAR

by Brian Chambouleyron

A dozen intermediate to advanced originals in notes & tab display various Latin American styles. For each, the CD features the lead part as well as an accompaniment-only rhythm track for play along.

00001123 Book/CD Pack $19.95

BEBOP GUITAR
Basic Theory and Practice for Jazz Guitar in the Style of Charlie Parker

by Joseph Weidlich

This book/CD pack shows guitarists how to transform basic jazz improv techniques into bebop figures in Bird's famous "with strings" style by making chromatic and rhythmic alterations. Includes many musical examples, most in the user-friendly key of G major, to accommodate players not well versed in jazz flat keys.

00001196 Book/CD Pack $25.95

GUITAR TUNING FOR THE COMPLETE MUSICAL IDIOT

by Ron Middlebrook

There's nothing more distracting than hearing a musician play out of tune. This user-friendly book/DVD pack teaches various methods for tuning guitars – even 12-strings! – and basses, including a section on using electronic tuning devices. Also covers intonation, picks, changing strings, and much more!

00000002 Book/DVD Pack........................$16.95
00001198 DVD $10.00

ASAP CLASSICAL GUITAR
Learn How to Play the Classical Way

by James Douglas Esmond

Teacher-friendly or for self-study, this book/CD pack for beginning to intermediate guitarists features classical pieces and exercises presented progressively in notes and tab, with each explained thoroughly and performed on the accompanying CD. A great way to learn to play ASAP!

00001202 Book/CD Pack $15.95

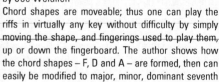

THE GUITAR CHORD SHAPES OF CHARLIE CHRISTIAN

by Joe Weidlich

Chord shapes are moveable; thus one can play the riffs in virtually any key without difficulty by simply moving the shape, and fingerings used to play them, up or down the fingerboard. The author shows how the chord shapes – F, D and A – are formed, then can easily be modified to major, minor, dominant seventh and diminished seventh chord voicings. The identifiable "sound" of a particular lick is preserved regardless of how many notes are added on either side of it, e.g., pickup notes or tag endings. Many examples are shown and played on the CD of how this basic concept was used by Charlie Christian.

00000388 Book/CD Pack $19.95

THE COUNTRY GUITAR STYLE OF CHARLIE MONROE
Based on the 1936-1938 Bluebird Recordings by The Monroe Brothers

by Joseph Weidlich

This great overview of Charlie Monroe's unique guitar performance style (he used just his thumb and index finger) presents 52 songs, with an in-depth look at the backup patterns & techniques from each chord family (G, F, D, C, E, A), plus special note sequences, common substitutions and stock backup phrases. Includes the bluegrass classics "Roll in My Sweet Baby's Arms," "My Long Journey Home" and "Roll On, Buddy," plus a discography and complete Bluebird recording session info.

00001305 ....$19.99

ASAP GUITARIST GUIDE TO STRING BENDING & VIBRATO
Learn How to Bend the Correct Way

by Dave Brewster

String bending and vibrato are two of the most popular guitar techniques used in all musical styles, yet for most beginning and intermediate players, gaining control of them might seem overwhelming. This book outlines some of the most common bending and vibrato techniques and licks, teaching them in an easy-to-digest manner to help you see and hear how to use them with confidence in a musical context. Contains more than 150 helpful examples!

00001347 Book/CD Pack $19.99

HYMNS AND SPIRITUALS FOR FINGERSTYLE GUITAR

by James Douglas Esmond

Originating in the South during the antebellum days on the old plantations, at religious revivals and at camp meetings, hymns and spirituals are the native folk songs of our own America. This collection features 13 songs, some with two arrangements – one easy, the second more difficult. Songs include: Were You There? • Steal Away • Amazing Grace • Every Time I Feel the Spirit • Wade in the Water • and more.

00001183 Book/CD Pack $19.95

P.O. Box 17878 - Anaheim Hills, CA 92817
(714) 779-9390   www.centerstream-usa.com

More Great Guitar Books from Centerstream...

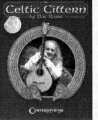